Music Minus One
VOCALS

SING 10 FAVORITES WITH SOUND-ALIKE
DEMO & BACKING TRACKS ONLINE

ELVIS PRESLEY

Cover photo © Bettmann / Getty Images

PLAYBACK+
Speed • Pitch • Balance • Loop

To access audio visit:
www.halleonard.com/mylibrary

Enter Code
2036-1987-8522-5386

ISBN: 978-1-5400-3150-1

ELVIS™ and ELVIS PRESLEY™ are trademarks of ABG EPE IP LLC
Rights of Publicity and Persona Rights: Elvis Presley Enterprises, LLC
© 2018 ABG EPE IP LLC
elvis.com

Visit Hal Leonard Online at
www.halleonard.com

Contact Us:
Hal Leonard
7777 West Bluemound Road
Milwaukee, WI 53213
Email: info@halleonard.com

In Europe contact:
Hal Leonard Europe Limited
Distribution Centre, Newmarket Road
Bury St Edmunds, Suffolk, IP33 3YB
Email: info@halleonardeurope.com

In Australia contact:
Hal Leonard Australia Pty. Ltd.
4 Lentara Court
Cheltenham, Victoria, 3192 Australia
Email: info@halleonard.com.au

ALL SHOOK UP

Words and Music by OTIS BLACKWELL
and ELVIS PRESLEY

DON'T BE CRUEL
(To a Heart That's True)

Words and Music by OTIS BLACKWELL
and ELVIS PRESLEY

Moderately fast

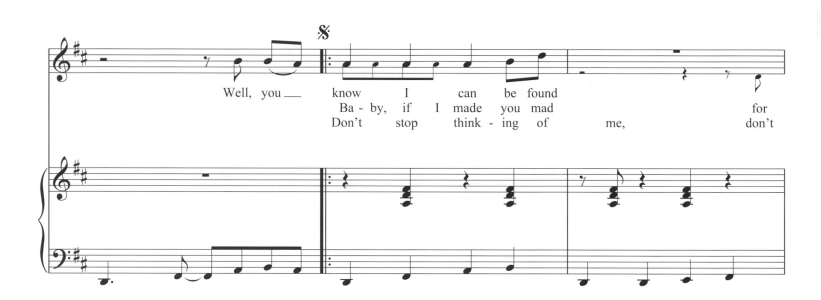

Well, you ___ know I can be found
Ba - by, if I made you mad
Don't stop think - ing of me, don't

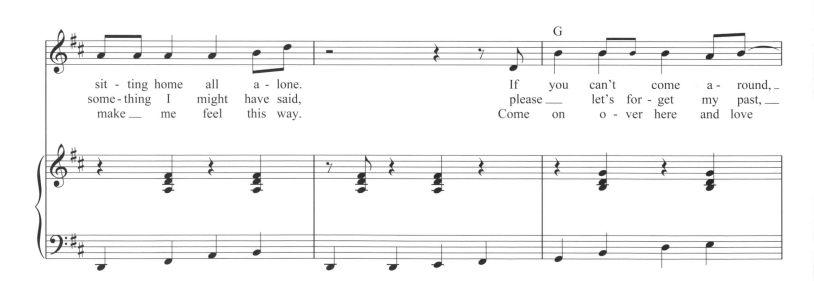

sit - ting home all a - lone.
some - thing I might have said,
make ___ me feel this way.

If you can't come a - round,___
please ___ let's for - get my past,
Come on o - ver here and love

BLUE SUEDE SHOES

Words and Music by
CARL LEE PERKINS

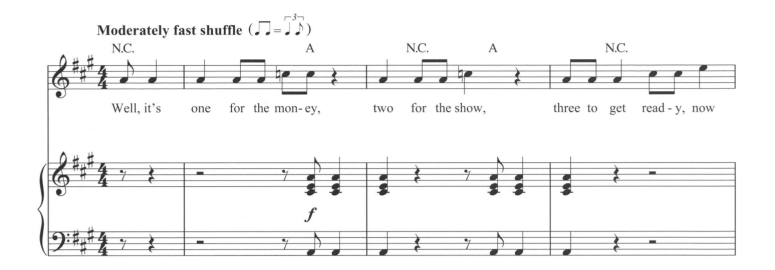

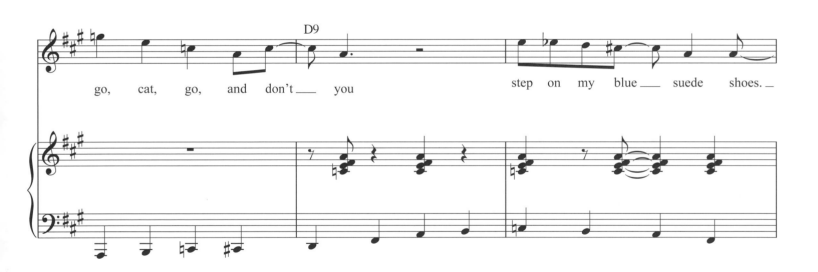

CAN'T HELP FALLING IN LOVE

Words and Music by GEORGE DAVID WEISS,
HUGO PERETTI and LUIGI CREATORE

Moderately slow ($\quad$ = 68)

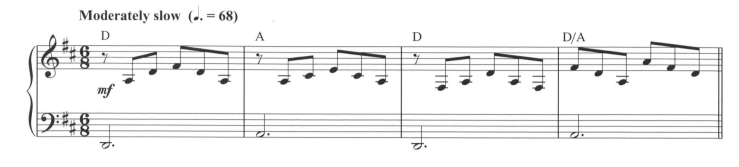

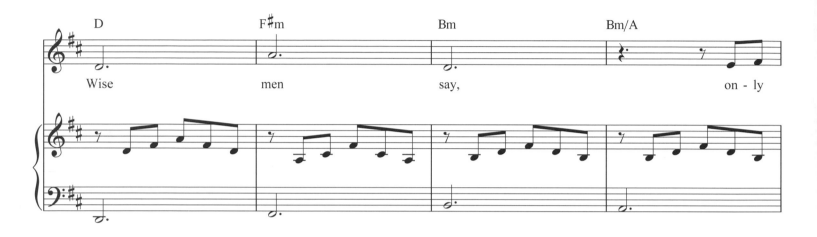

Wise   men   say,   on - ly

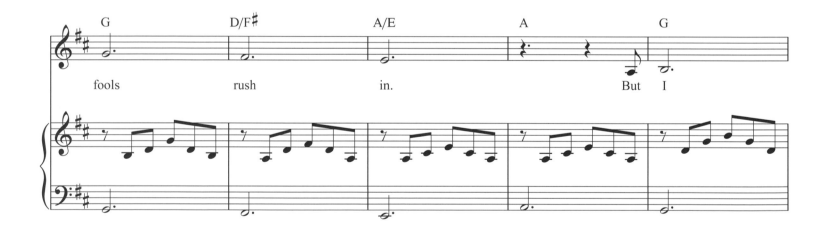

fools   rush   in.   But   I

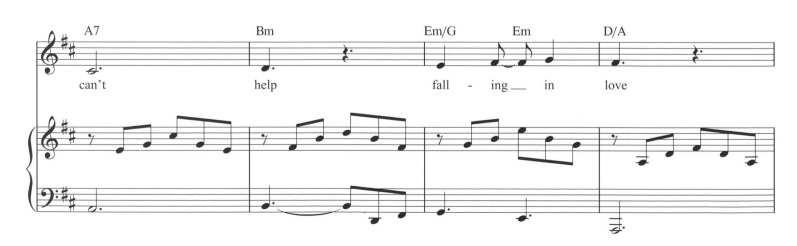

can't   help   fall - ing __ in love

HOUND DOG

Words and Music by JERRY LEIBER
and MIKE STOLLER

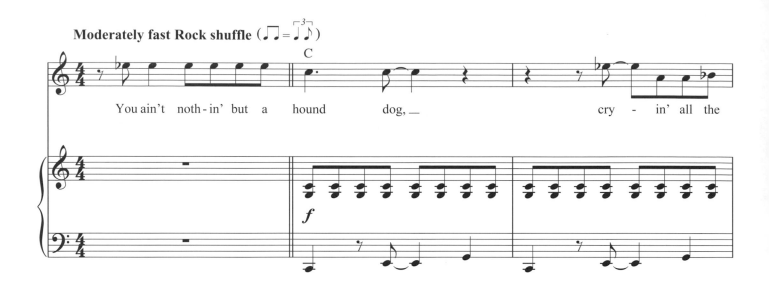

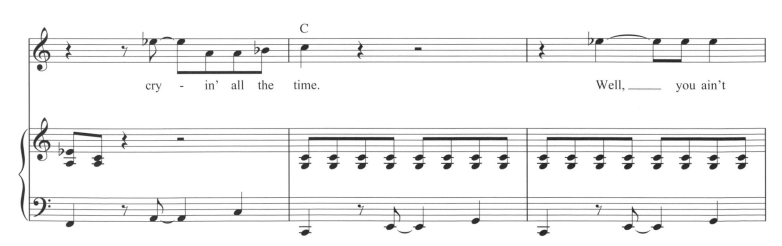

nev - er caught a rab - bit and you ain't no friend of mine. ___

Guitar solo ad lib.

(Solo ends) Well, they said you was high ___ classed.

Well, that was just a lie.   Yeah, they said   you was high___

___ classed.   Well,   that   was just a   lie.

Well,___   you ain't   nev - er caught a   rab - bit   and you   ain't   no   friend   of   mine.___

You ain't   noth - in' but a

IT'S NOW OR NEVER

Words and Music by AARON SCHROEDER
and WALLY GOLD

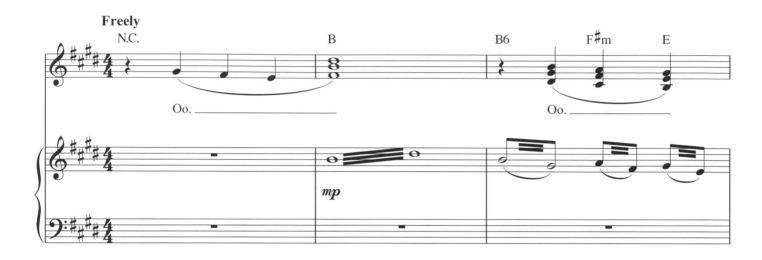

JAILHOUSE ROCK

Words and Music by JERRY LEIBER
and MIKE STOLLER

LOVE ME TENDER

Words and Music by ELVIS PRESLEY
and VERA MATSON

Gentle Ballad

Love me _____ ten - der, love me sweet, _____
Love me _____ ten - der, love me long, _____
Love me _____ ten - der, love me dear, _____

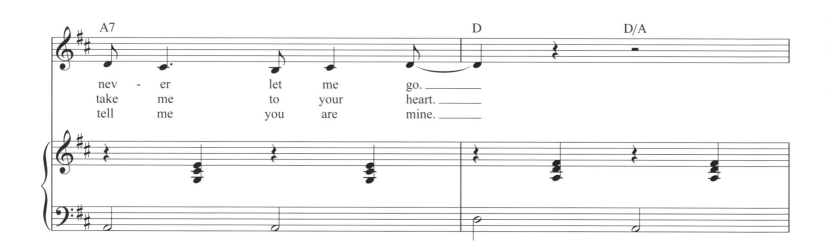

nev - er let me go. _____
take me to your heart. _____
tell me you are mine. _____

You have made _____ my life _____ com - plete,
For it's there _____ that I _____ be - long
I'll be yours _____ through all _____ the years,

SUSPICIOUS MINDS

Words and Music by
FRANCIS ZAMBON

RETURN TO SENDER

Words and Music by OTIS BLACKWELL
and WINFIELD SCOTT

46